GENEALOGY OF THE FAMILY OF ST. GREGORY

Illuminator of Armenia, and the life of Nerses, Patriarch of Armenia

St. Mesrop Mashtots,

Translated by: D.P. Curtin

Dalcassian Publishing Company

PHILADELPHIA, PA

Copyright @ 2023 Dalcassian Publishing Company

All rights reserved. No part of this publication may be reproduced, distributed, or transmitted in any form or by any means, including photocopying, recording, or other electronic or mechanical methods, without the prior written permission of the publisher, except in the case of brief quotations embodied in critical reviews and certain other non-commercial uses permitted by copyright law. For permission request, write to Dalcassian Publishing Company at dalcassianpublishing at gmail.com

ISBN: 979-8-8690-6061-7 (Paperback)

Library of Congress Control Number:
Author: Curtin, D.P. (1985-)

Printed by Ingram Content Group, 1 Ingram Blvd, La Vergne, Tennessee

First printing edition 2023.

Ս. ՄԵՍՐՈՊ

Genealogy of the Family of St. Gregory, Illuminator of Armenia,
and the life of St. Nerses, Patriarch of Armenia

I. In the eighteenth year [of the reign] of the great Tiridates, the seat of the apostle Thaddeus was occupied by Gregory, illuminator of Armenia, who led the entire country to the knowledge of the truth of Christ. Several years later, he took his place among the angels. The shepherds who found him dead at the foot of the mountain, not having recognized him, buried him and covered his grave with stones. During his lifetime, he had consecrated his son Arisdagues as his successor.

GENEALOGY OF THE FAMILY OF ST. GREGORY

During the fall of the Arsacid dynasty, the country of Armenia was divided between the Persians and the Greeks. The emperor (king) who then reigned over the Greeks sent Perinte (Berindianos?) as a general of Mesopotamia. At that time, the relics of the holy Illuminator of Armenia having been found, the Emperor of the Greeks, Zeno, was informed, who sent many legionaries, under the orders of the general of Mesopotamia, who arrived and seized by force the relics of St. Gregory. He gave his right hand with another fragment to the Armenians, because Gregory had enlightened them first, and he brought [the body] whole with some relics of the Hripsimian saints to Constantinople, where they were placed in the same tomb.

St. Rhesdagus was bishop of Greater Armenia for seven years, and was killed by an Armenian called Archelaus, from the canton of Dzop. The body of Rhesdagues was transported to the canton of Egéghiatz, in the village of Thil, and they buried him there. His elder brother Verthanes succeeded him. In his time, the general of Armenia, Vatche, lord of the Mamigonians, died in a great battle. St. Verthanes dedicated a memento for him in the salutary mass, and founded, for the intention of Vatché the Mamigonian and the other soldiers who had died in the battle, a mass which the Armenians still say to this day. Then Verthanes died in peace and his body was placed in the village of Thortan. He was patriarch of Great Armenia for fifteen years. After him, the seat was occupied by the young Jousig, grandson of Verthanes. Jousig had two sons, Bab and Athenogenes (Athanakines). Jousig, seeing that his sons had dissolute morals and were not worthy of the priesthood, fell into deep sadness and remained inconsolable. Always worried and tormented about them, he never stopped praying to God. Now, one night, the angel of the Lord appeared to him and said to him: "Jousig, do not be sad because of your sons who have made themselves unworthy of the priesthood. There will be born to your son a child who will renew the heritage of the holy apostle Thaddeus and consolidate the seat of the great patriarch Gregory, the Illuminator of Armenia, and he will be called Nerses. From him will flow the graces of God's commandments; God will grant him a great rest, and churches will be built; he will convert many lost and ignorant people into the Lord. Thus, Christ will be glorified by many mouths, by those who will be the pillars of faith and the distributors of the word of life. These will cultivate many perennial plants, productive and useful branches in the spiritual paradise, and which will be piled up in the stores of God. More than once they will be persecuted because of the commandments of the Lord, but they will remain steadfast like a rock. When they are dead, lies will rule with insolent, selfish, greedy, deceitful, ungodly and ambitious men. The impiety of that time will be so great that the faithful will have difficulty remaining firm [in the faith]."

Jousig, having heard these words from the mouth of the angel, was consoled and thanked the Lord for having judged him worthy of this revelation. Then Jousig married his son Athenogenes and gave him as wife the sister of King Diran, who was called Pampischen. She had a son who was born under happy auspices and who was named Nerses, as the angel had announced. Then Jousig was martyred by Diran and died. His body was taken and placed in the tomb of his father Verthanes in Thortan. For six years he occupied the seat of Great Armenia. However, as there was no one from the family of St. Gregory to occupy the patriarchate, they chose, as patriarch of Great Armenia, a certain Pharnersèh who occupied the seat for four years - After the death of the one Here, the seat of Armenia was vacant for a year.

II. The young Nerses grew up and learned in the province of Caesarea, having with him his wife Santoukhd, of the race of the Mamigonians, by whom he had a son whom he named Sahag. Three years later Santoukhd died in Caesarea; his father Vartan the Mamigonian transported his body to the town of Thil and buried him there.

After this, Arsaces [III] (Arschag) ruled in place of his father Diran [II]. Nerses came close to him and was named chamberlain (responsible for guarding) all his treasure, because he was a cousin of King Arsaces. However, the country of Armenia, from the death of Jousig until the [advent] of Nerses the Great, all, great and small, had strayed from the ways of God and surrendered themselves to all kinds of debauchery, like in Sodom. This is why God abandoned them without help and delivered them into the hands of their enemies who inflicted cruel torments on them. Then the religious of the country having gathered together learned, through the spirit of prophecy, that there would be no salvation for Armenia if a pastor of the race of St. Gregory was not found. One of the great satraps of the canton of Schirag, of the Kenouni race, named Barkèv, who had retired to the mountains, presented himself and said [as if by an inspiration] of divine providence: "I have saw at the king's palace a young man from the family of St. Gregory, called Nerses, of mature age, and full of wisdom and the graces of God." At this news, joy was extreme, because, by the hand of Nerses, God was going to save the country of Armenia, as in fact happened.

Arsace, seeing that there was no spiritual leader among the descendants of the holy family of the great patriarch Gregory, nor a general of the brave and noble family of the Mamigonians, and knowing above all that the ruin of the country of Armenia was due to this absence, he himself set out at the head of his army, in order to go in search of the brave and faithful family of the Mamigonians whose members were the nourishers, the masters and familiars of the king. He met them in the canton of Daïk, their country, having with them the Kenouni, and he brought them back with him. Indeed, at the time of Diran's reign, they had left the [king's] entourage, the command of the army and all the affairs of Armenia. The race of the Mamigonians then consisted of four brothers, called: Vartan, Vasag, Vahan and Vrouj, all sons of Ardavazd, son of Vasché the Mamigonian. The king appointed them generals of Great Armenia which, at all times, had been subject to the first kings. He invests Vasag with the command-in-chief of the army of Armenia, in order to lead in the fighting, and placed three brothers under his command, with the title of Chilearch (hazarabed). These Mamigonians thus became generals; they fought and put to flight the armies drawn up in array. They drew the bow and carried the eagle; their spears and their shields threw lightning: they had a heart.

proof, never weakening in fights; they were intrepid in the fray, justly renowned for their valor, and flying their banners from the shafts of their spears. As soon as the faithful family of the Mamigonians had been called to command the army, they were all seen flying into battle, like the fire that swirls among the reeds.

III. After this, the country of Armenia and King Arsaces held council [relating to divine things], and particularly to the family of St. Gregory. The satraps and the great ones of Armenia, the races and the parents [of the king], the standard-bearers of the lords of all ranks, the governors of the provinces, the generals, the guards of the borders, the bishops, the priests and all the multitude of the people gathered together at the king's house, and having all agreed, they said to king Arsaces: "Since God has renewed through you the throne of the Arsaids and the chief command of the troops in the illustrious family of the

Mamigonians, it is also necessary to restore the patriarchal seat by the race of St. Gregory, in order to purify and illuminate the morals of Armenia." The king replied: "This question also concerns me." Then the whole crowd pointed out by name the young Nerses, son of Athenogenes, son of Jousig, son of Verthanes, son of St. Gregory. In his childhood, he had been raised and instructed by faithful masters and he had married to give a successor to the [patriarchal] seat, after having lived for three years with his chaste wife Santoukhd of the family of the Mamigonians, he had Sahag. On the death of his wife, he came to his relative King Arsaces, who appointed him his chamberlain and his advisor for royal affairs. Nerses was tall; he had a pleasant face, and his appearance was imposing; he feared God and cared for the poor. He requested the king's mercy for the oppressed and slandered people, and he took charge of feeding the orphans and widows. He wore the ring with the king's seal.

All the people were looking for Nerses to put him at the head of the patriarchal see of Armenia. When he was brought into the presence of the king and heard the acclamations of the people, he stood in the midst of the crowd and began to falsely accuse himself of sins and impiety, [saying] that he was unworthy of the ministry. The crowd, having heard these words, raised a clamor and said: "This sinner and this unworthy man will be our pastor and our spiritual leader; he must ascend the seat of the apostle St. Thaddeus and the great patriarch Gregory." They seized him; but he again repeated: "You place, as mediator between God and men, a sinner who has committed a multitude of crimes, and I tell you this so that you may be ashamed. You hold my life in your hands, but I am not worthy of the honor you give me. May God give you a superior and a leader according to your hope!" Having heard these words, the crowd understood that it was out of fear of God that he spoke like this. Then they all, with the king, cried out together: "Let your sins be upon us and on our heads; may your actions fall on us and on our children! But accept from us the [spiritual ministry which is the inheritance] of your fathers."

Seeing that he could no longer object, because the crowd persisted [in its resolution], Nerses began to reproach the soldiers: "You are impious and cowards who hate your masters; infidels, murderers of your masters; you are hardened criminals, informers, enemies of your friends; you are traitors to your masters and rebels. No, I cannot become your pastor, because today you love me without reason, and tomorrow you will hate me; I will be an enemy to you and I will become a club that you call upon your heads. How can I lift up my hands to God to pray for a nation whose murderous hands are stained with the blood of the innocent? how can I become the leader of a nation that has abandoned the Lord God?" Nerses said all this and other things in front of the king, the princes and the immense crowd of people. The king, astonished, remained silent. Then Nerses said again: "Let me live in peace, according to my position and my sins, while awaiting the punishment which will follow the judgment."

The assembly then continued: "Forgive us our sins as your master [Jesus Christ] forgave his executioners, for we have not sinned against you, as they sinned against Him who was their master. And you, all are content as you are, become our pastor."

This great insistence on the part of the people was an effect of God's providence. The king got up and ordered Nerses to be carefully watched over during the night until morning, lest he escape. That same night, the angel of the Lord appeared to Nerses and said to him: "Do not refuse to accept this [spiritual] direction, for the Lord wills it this way." He then replied: "May the will of the Lord be done!" The next day, King Arsaces had Nerses brought into his presence, and, in front of the assembly, he stood up all irritated, took away his steel sword with the sheath adorned with precious stones, which Nerses wore for the service of the king. He ordered him to be bound and to take off the garment that the king had given him.

Then the king ordered a bishop of a respectable age, named Festus (Phesdos), to be called, to bring priestly vestments, to clothe Nerses with them, and he had him consecrated deacon. His curly hair was cut, which formed a crown around his head. Seeing this, many people began to shed tears, because no one could match her in beauty. However, when they saw divine grace manifested in him, they rejoiced, for they understood that it was to him that the words of the angel to Jousig applied: "From your son will be born a son who will be a vessel chosen by the nations; he will mount the seat of Thaddeus; he will occupy the place of his fathers, the first patriarchs, and he will indicate the path of life." We knew that it was God who had designated him, which is why the people, inspired by God, insisted.

After that, several detachments of troops and bishops were assembled to take blessed Nerses to Caesarea, where [the Armenians] were in the habit of having their patriarchs consecrated. The king, it is said, formed an escort to accompany Nerses. [It consisted of] general Schahèn of the family of the Mamigonians and other princes from each of the provinces: David, prince of the Bagratides (Pakradouni); Hemaïag, prince of Khorkhoruni; Sahag, prince of the Ardzrouni; Manèdj, prince of the Kénouni; Tigrane (Dikran), prince of the Varajnouni; Vatclié, prince of the Amadouni; of the chiefs of the cantons of the country, Moujegh, prince of Daron; Vezroug, prince of the Iberians (Virk); Vrèn, prince of Koghtèn; Varen, prince of the house of Makhaz; Haif, from the house of Martbed (eunuchs), who are called the king's father; Makhaz, prince of the Antzévatzi; Zarèh, prince of Mog; Moujan, prince of Aghdznik; Méhentag, prince of Reschdouni; Varazt Schahouni, prince of Dzop; Vagharsch, prince of Antzid; Varazvaghan, prince of Kapéglnan; Knith, prince of Hashdian; Sak, prince of Parmi; Antoug, prince of Siounie; Manavaz, prince of the country of Dzor (valley); Ardag, prince of Harkh; Arschavir, prince of the house of Angegh; Kazrig, prince of Daik. These were accompanied by the bishops of the most important sees: Gregory, bishop of Siounie; Pharen, bishop of the Iberians; Thathoul, bishop of Daron; Joseph, bishop of the Bagradites (Pakradouni); Khatchatch, bishop of the house of Martbed; Amos, bishop of Peznouni; Nerses, bishop of Mog; Sapor (Schabouh), bishop of Ardzrouni; Absalon (Apésoghom), bishop of Antzévatzi; Vahan, bishop of the Mamigonians; Zavèn, bishop of Tzerdav; Tiridates, bishop of Pasèn; Knel, bishop of Melitene. Still other bishops, fifteen in number, prepared [to leave] with the princes, as well as other governors and chiefs of the cantons of the country of Armenia, carrying with them the letter of King Arsaces and his presents.

Nerses was made to mount with great pomp in the royal chariot drawn by white mules, and he was given four thousand horsemen as an escort. People from the countryside, seeing them coming from afar, fled, believing they were dealing with a troop of enemies. However, when they recognized them, the princes of the cantons gave them a great welcome. But they did not want to stop in several places, and they arrived at the borders of the Cappadocians (Kamirk), in the metropolis of Caesarea. They appeared before the great bishop Eusebius, gave him the letter from King Aisace, and presented Nerses to him.

The blessed bishop received them with great honors and testimonies of friendship; then, according to the precepts of the apostles, he immediately brought together a large number of bishops from the regions of Greece, in order to consecrate with pomp, the great Nerses as catholicos of Great Armenia, which was the share of the apostle Thaddeus.

When we entered the church, a great miracle was manifested: a white dove descended from heaven in a material form, and alighted on the holy altar, in the eyes of all the clergy and the considerable crowd of people. There was an archpriest of the church of Caesarea called Basil, on whom the dove hovered as it fluttered above him. When Nerses mounted the seat, the dove took flight and came to rest on the head of Nerses, and it remained there until the end of the holy ordination. While this miracle was taking place, the Patriarch Eusebius himself remained plunged in great astonishment which lasted several hours. All the people then cried out: "This man is worthy of the patriarchy, because the Spirit of God rested on him, as before on the Savior at the Jordan, and on the Apostles in the upper room." The crowd grew [in the Church] and the Armenian soldiers, who were with St. Nerses, had difficulty containing it. The hour having arrived, the holy patriarch Nerses celebrated mass; from a distance a column of fire was seen descending from the two onto the church, at the very place where Nerses was officiating; we also heard the voices of the celestial troops who accompanied him singing praises thrice holy. When the mass was over, they went to the banquet, and the face of the great Nerses beamed like that of the chief of the prophets, Moses, on the mountain. At this sight, the astonishment of the spectators increased still further.

Following these miracles, and [after having received] magnificent presents and gifts from the Greek princes and the blessed bishop Eusebius, the escort of the Armenians set out. on the way with his patriarch. When the inhabitants of the lands of the Greeks and Syrians knew of the miracles which had taken place in the person of the great Nerses, they began to follow him to receive his blessing. They presented themselves to him, saying: "This is the man whom the Holy Spirit, in the form of a dove, declared to be a true patriarch." Many lepers, cripples, sick and possessed people were brought to his feet, who received their healing from his hand; and all the populations congratulated the country of Armenia, because of this holy man.

GENEALOGY OF THE FAMILY OF ST. GREGORY

In Sebaste, St. Nerses stopped in several places, and had many churches built. Eight princes were immediately sent to King Arsaces to inform him of the arrival of Nerses. These princes were: the prince of Ankegh, the prince of Dzop, the prince of the Arscharouni, the prince of the Bagratides, the prince of Antzid, the prince of the Ardzrouni, the prince of the Mamigoniens, and the prince of the Reschdouni, who met the king in the province of Ararat. King Arschag, accompanied by these princes and an immense crowd, came to meet St. Nerses, as far as the mountain of Arioutz (the Lion). The king and the patriarch met, and the country of the Armenians rejoiced. Nerses was taken and placed on the seat of the apostle Thaddeus and his ancestor Gregory. Thus were renewed the seat and heritage of Great Armenia and the race of Azkanaz.

IV. St. Nerses worked and taught according to the word of the Gospel, and he devoted himself to doing good for Armenia.

I must say why the Armenians sought consecration in Caesarea. When the country of Armenia fell to the apostle Thaddeus, he first came to King Abgar in Edessa (Urlia), and he illuminated the country. But as Caesarea had always been under the domination of the Armenians, the apostle Thaddeus also went to that country, and when he had converted [the inhabitants], he ordained one of his disciples priest and bishop, named after Théophile, whom he established as spiritual leader; then he went to Armenia. It is for this reason that the Armenians went to ask for their consecration in Caesarea until the Council of Chalcedon.

V. After being consecrated at Caesarea, the great Nerses returned to Armenia and renewed the investiture of Armenian princes which had been established by Chosroes (Khosrov) and the other kings; then he established the order [of precedence] at the table of King Arsaces. There were four hundred seats, namely: the Haïgazni; the Barthevians (Parthians); the Araradian (Araratiens); the Pakradouni (Bagratids); the Dikranouni (Tigranians); the Asbédouni; the Makhazouni; the Khorkhorouni; the Ardzrouni; the Mamigonians; the Siounians; the Amadouni; the Ankéghians; the Iberians (Virk); the Dzops; the Varajnouni; the Martbedouni; the Vahévouni; the Bahlavouni; the Gasp (Caspians); the Sisanesen; the Gatmian; the Manavazian; the Etesians (Edessians); the Kamrian (Cappadocians); the Peznouni; the Sasanians (Sasanians); the Kishons; the Aegean; the Iiavbédouni; the Antzdiai; the

GENEALOGY OF THE FAMILY OF ST. GREGORY

Sébasdians; the Ashdischadians; the Srouantzdiaï; the Antzavatzi; the Asbaknouni; the Resch(.louni; the Vahanounij the Aglitzaian; the Khogliian; the Gazpouni; the Gamsaragan; the Mogalzi; the Segbgouni j the Rhenthouni; the Aderbadouni; the Koghténiaï; the Kazpigan; the Dzogligerd; the Makliazian; the Mrovouni; the Rasmouni; the Kapéghian; the Sbarouni; the Vahouni; the Vrendcliouni; the Soudan; the Timagsian; the Srouni; the Tarpantian; the Arakatzian; the Gokovdian; the Abaliouni; the Entzaïnotz; the Herkhian; the Gortovaï; the Aravéghian; the Hasclidian; the Vrian; the Vanantian; the Pharadjouni; the Daschiratz; the Ourtziaï; the Mantagouni; the Daï; the Mélidian; the Taschdgadn; the Pasèn; the Dzaghgouni; the second Mamigonians; the Pherejouni; the Delkhian; the Pakovan; the Aschdotzian; the Apéghouni; the Khaldian; the Sabarouni; the Asckhakodan the Kenouni; the Hamazkouni; the Agiai; the Vijouni; the Aropsouni; the Sehaborabed; the Dzaïthiouni; the Zanahdjirabed; the Varazadagian; the Entzaïeni; the Meghrouni; the Arscliouni; the Khadan; the Martaghians; the Légantians; the Kliordzeni: the Tzivnagan; the Hamoutzians; the Gorthians; the Geghounti; the Zarévlians; the Dourpéranians; the Pjouni; the Depkhouni; the Mehrouni; the Khagbakliabed; the Gaïouschian; the Sbantouni; the Ardaschadians; the Orsabeds; the lords of Arkhadzotz; the Rapsians; the Pakrasbouni; the Barsbouni; the Agliegbnatrosch; the Kertcliouni; the Nedogh; the Namagouni; the Khaghovians; the Asbarakliaghs; the Aprahamians; the Husnagans; the Pagliasagans; the Dighp; the Liarnagans; the Sabrasamians; the Hedjmadag; the Koroghovaïs; the Varteschians; the Tramants; the Khatchians; the Khagbpians; the Trosehagirs; the Makhalouni; the Osgémani; the Aroujian; the Gaghardch; the Dathévians; the Tadavdjir; the Dzorapnag; the Djagadamough; the Terdchain; the Sclialiabouni; the Among Ai; the Gamkhiaï; the Kavarabed.

There were still others who did not have seats: the Louribian; the Pokliaïouni; the Movatzians; the Abegouni; the Kbnouni, the Paznouni; the Aghnévouni; the Yuranians; the Geznouni; the Douscliouni; the Gi'ouni; the Maznouni; the Makhazouni.

Here is the list of seats with others that I found unnecessary to write down. They were confirmed by King Arsaces, who had four hundred seats placed at the table, according to the order of the great Nerses. The clergy, divided into nine classes, sat behind them.

VI. Before the ordination of the great Nerses, cenobites, bishops and solitaries lived with their families in towns and villages, which he found unseemly and contrary to ecclesiastical discipline. After that, the great Nerses soon passed into Georgia, in the inheritance of the Apostle Nino; from there he went to the country of the Greeks and to the borders of the Persians. He gave the order to build bishoprics and convents large and small, and he also ordered the construction of hostels in less frequented places, at the bends of the roads, on the tops of the mountains, and hospitals in cities and countryside. He had the tombs of kings, princes and generals erected in monasteries, so that the religious could take care of them in common. He gave villages and farms to convents for their maintenance. At the time of Nerses, no beggars were seen in the country of Armenia. There were still in Armenia, for many years, reprehensible customs and unfortunate injustices which were abolished by St. Nerses. Lepers, who were called people with ulcers or scabies, were chased out of populated areas so that their illness would not be transmitted to others. These unfortunate people therefore moved away from their parents or their brothers, their fathers or their wives, and this was a great cause of trouble. Many fell prey to wild beasts, others were drowned in rivers, others were swallowed up by snow and were lost forever. The great Nerses brought them all back to their homes and forbade their expulsion, as had happened before. Then, by an inspiration of the Holy Spirit, he gathered them together in the canton of Antzevatzi, at the place where there was the image of the Mother of God which had been brought to Armenia by the apostle Bartholomew, and where a church had been raised under his invocation. Lepers found cure for their illnesses there and other infirm people were also healed. St. Nerses established a pilgrimage in this place, which is made to this day for the glory of God, and there we find healing for leprosy.

For twenty-five years, Nerses traveled through the various provinces which were placed under his jurisdiction. There he established and propagated the rules of the Holy Church, which filled the Armenians with joy. Many people from among the pagans came to Armenia and were baptized there.

Now it happened that, while Nerses was visiting the very fertile province of Ararat, he met there the martbed (chief of the eunuchs), called the father of the king. Seeing the large villages with which Nerses had endowed his convent, the chief of the eunuchs became jealous and said: "I will warn the king and I will take these domains for the court." Nerses, having heard him, said to him: "Since you have uttered threats, you will not reach the king." When he left, the chief of the eunuchs, Haïr, met a prince of the Ardzrouni who killed him while he was hunting. Thus the word of the man of God, St. Nerves, was fulfilled; and everyone admired the prompt execution of his prediction.

The Armenians had also preserved pagan habits. Thus, when a person died, they tore their faces in despair; blood flowed in abundance, and this is how they accompanied their dead. In addition, they married between relatives and consanguineous relatives, as a result of their impiety and with a view to propagating their own race. The great Nerses abolished this custom in Armenia and defended marriage between relatives up to the fifth degree. At the time of Blessed Nerses, all of Armenia formed a single family, because he gave himself as an example to the whole country as a pastor whose life never caused scandal.

Vile. After this, it happened that Antog, prince of Siounie, had a daughter named Pharandzem who was given in marriage to Knel the Arsacid, cousin of King Arsaces. Her reputation for beauty spread throughout the country, because there was no woman so beautiful, so modest and passionately loving her husband. When Dirith, cousin of Arsace, saw his sister-in-law Pharandzem, he fell in love with her and sought all means to lose young Knel, and to be able to marry Pharandzem. Dirith joined forces with other evil men who slandered him to the king, saying: "Young Knel came to assassinate you. "The king believed these denunciations and he meditated in his heart the plan to kill young Knel; however, he did not dare to do it publicly for fear of St. Nerses.

On the feast of St. John, the Precursor (Garabed) which had been instituted by Gregory the Illuminator, we met in the canton of Kami in Scliahabivan. The king's troop was also there, and the great Nerses was also brought there to celebrate the festival. That day, young Knel also came there with his whole family. Now, when the king was informed of his coming, he sent armed troops to meet him, carrying swords, hidden among infantrymen with only their shields. As soon as they had reached him, [the soldiers] made young Knel dismount, tied his hands behind his back and led him to execution. His wife Pharandzem, seeing this, cried out and ran to find St. Nerses who was celebrating the office and had not yet finished the morning prayers. Pharandzem came near him and told him the fate reserved for her husband. She kissed the feet of St. Nerses and, wetting them with her tears, she said: "Alas! I am lost, have pity on me, holy archbishop! The young Knel that you love, my husband, will be taken from me without having committed any fault! Blessed be God, I will not leave your feet until you show my innocent husband, young Knel, to my darkened eyes. Come without delay, holy patriarch, come at once, for the young branch is separated from the vine; come at once, for the righteous are sacrificed with iniquity; come quickly, holy patriarch; comes to the aid of Knel who is abandoned; come quickly, holy man of God, for the innocent sheep is among the wolves; she is troubled, and she is without hope; there is no shepherd who can help this young man, and the animals have no pity on him!"

St, Nerses began to shed tears, interrupted the morning service and hastily went to the king in the royal residence. Pharandzem carried his clothes and his staff so that he could hasten further. St. Nerses ordered her to wait for him, lest the king, in love with her beauty, would not listen to her intercession on behalf of Knel. When St. Nerses was seen coming into the camp, everyone left their tent and came to meet the patriarch, who was crossing the ranks to arrive in all haste near the king. The king, having learned that he was coming to intercede in favor of Knel, so that he might be spared his life, immediately covered his face as if he were sleeping and turned on his side, so as not to hear the prayers. of St. Nerses and give [his executioners] time to assassinate Knel. St. Nerses shook him by the hands on his throne and drew him towards him; but the king let himself go like the dead and closed his eyes. Then St. Nerses immediately got up, and, hurrying like a courier, he himself ran to come to the aid of Knel and ordered a horse to be brought to him. As soon as we arrived at the camp, the chief of the executioners immediately arrived who entered saying: "We, I and those who accompanied me, have executed the king's order; we killed young Knel on the small hill near the wall of the wild animal reserve."

At this news, the great Nerses, overwhelmed with sadness, ran to the king's residence and said to him: "Unjust king, you covered your ears with your hands, imitating the serpent and the asp who withdraw into themselves to escape the charmers; but this means does not save them. You did the same and you did not spare your cousin (brother's son), your companion and your close relative. But he who became our brother on his own will not spare you on the day of your punishment. You murdered Knel because of the succession to the throne; but your kingship will be divided like that of Israel and your domains will be divided by foreigners, your enemies. You will be given over to slavery, to famine, to the sword and to the yoke of servitude [which will always weigh] on your neck. Your property and your country will fall prey to foreigners, and you will flee at the mere rustling of the leaves. You will be despised like corrupted water and you will no longer have the strength to bend a bow. Race of the Arsacids! you will empty the chalice to the dregs and you will get drunk with it; you will fall and never get up again. God will leave you to your own devices for a while for the good of the country; after which he will take away from you the kingship and the priesthood, and you will walk in the world without leaders, like a flock deprived of its shepherd. As for you who murdered your brother Knel, you have renewed the crime of Cain and you will be burdened under the same curses; During your lifetime, the kingship will be taken away from you and you will experience even more sorrow than your father Diran. You will kill yourself with the sword, like Saul and Herod, and you will depart from life by a cruel death." St. Nerses uttered these words with others, and the ashamed king fixed his eyes on the ground, as if struck by dizziness. The great Nerses left and did not appear again in the king's camp. He traveled through the cantons of Vasbheure and re-established the institutions of the Church there. From there, he headed towards Iberia, and he restored many churches there. However, the wife of young Knel began to lament in the royal camp; she mourned bitterly the loss of her husband and brought tears to the eyes of all those present. Dirith sent a messenger to say to him: "Do not cry like this, for you will be my wife." When Pharandzem heard it, she began to lament and say: "Men, listen, it is because of me that my husband was killed."

King Arsaces, rushing to the cries of Pharandzem, saw her and was in love with her beauty. Upon learning of this, Dirith fled, so as not to be put to death by the lord who sent soldiers after him. They reached him and killed him in the province of Daïk. Arsace married Pharandzem who gave him two sons, the first of whom was called Bab and the second Tiridates (Dertad).

The murderers of Knel died, thanks to the prayers of St. Nerses, who said: "The hands which have dipped in blood, and the tongues which have slandered Knel before the king, will not be covered with blessed earth, but they will be [deprived of burial] until the arrival of the judge who will do them justice." According to the word of the man of God, their bodies are preserved until now in caves of difficult access in the province of Karni.

VIII. However, Pharandzem hated King Arsaces and spoke to him haughtily. King Arsace, seeing the hatred [that his wife bore him], sent [messengers] to Greece and had the sister of the emperor (king) Valens (Vaghes) brought to him as his wife, who was called Olympia (Oghonibis). The king gave her the crown, because he preferred her to Pharandzem. Pharandzem immediately conceived hatred against Olympia and sought to destroy her. She found an accomplice in the person of a palace priest named Merdchounig, who committed an incredible crime. He mixed poison with the invigorating drink, with the salutary mystery [of the Eucharist]; he gave it to Queen Olympia in the church, and thus murdered her.

When the emperor [of the Greeks] learned of the death of his sister, he wanted to start war between the Armenians and the Greeks. When king Arsaces learned that the king of the Persians Sapor (Scliabouh) and the emperor of the Greeks had joined forces against him, he went in person with his army in search of the great patriarch Nerses [who was] in Ashdischad, in [the canton of] Daron. The king threw himself at the feet of St. Nerses, he asked him for forgiveness for his faults and [promised him] to be faithful according to his will. The bishops and princes of the country also begged him not to abandon the country entrusted to him. The saint agreed to make peace, and everyone decided that St. Nerses, accompanied by satraps, would go to the emperor of the Greeks, Valens, in order to renew the alliance of the great kings, St. Constantine, St. Tiridates, and our Illuminator St. Gregory, had concluded between themselves.

Then we prepared and provided [with the necessary things] the most illustrious satraps of Armenia. They were Vartan Mamigonien, brother of Vasag; Kardchogh Makhaz (with deadly weapons), satrap of Khorkhorouni; Mouschgan, satrap of the Sahrouni; Ivnel, satrap of the Kénouni; Geschgen, satrap of Parne; Méhévan, satrap of the Antzevatzi; Méhentag, satrap of the Reschdouni; Sourig, satrap of the Kapéghen; Meliroujan, satrap of the Ardzrouni; Pakrat, satrap of the Bagratids; Vrèn, satrap of the Iberians: Khoujèn, satrap of Dzoph; Sbantiad, satrap of Melitene; Dzamag, satrap of Haschdiank; Makouk, satrap of Adherbadagan; Vezroug, satrap of Pasèn; Retès, satrap of the Iberians; Hate the Martbed. All went with St. Nerses to an embassy to the imperial court, with a view to making friends and renewing the alliance which existed between the Armenians and the Greeks.

Emperor Valens first showered many honors on the satraps of Great Armenia, and he placed the seat of the great Nerses above those of the metropolitans and patriarchs, because St. Nerses had been distinguished by God. Every day the emperor increased for them [the testimonies] of friendship and honor. However, Emperor Valens was infected with the wicked heresy of Arius; he confessed that the Son is not the equal of the Father, that he had been begotten by the Father before time, that he was a foreign being, created, inferior and formed after time; that the holy Virgin Mary was not Mother of God, but mother of man, according to Macedonius who fought against the divinity of the Holy Spirit, of whom he said that he was not God and was not going to be worshiped or glorified with the Father, that he was not a divine person, but that he was foreign to the nature of God the Father, having received his existence from another and being only the servant and the minister, and finally having only a secondary influence.

Valens had a son called Trajan (Draïanos) who was the only heir to the empire, and the only representative of his race. Sometime later, Trajan fell ill with a serious illness. The emperor forced St. Nerses to pray over the child, so that he would escape death. But St. Nerses said to the emperor: "If you recognize the Son as God begotten by God and not created, co-eternal with the Father and then born of the Virgin Mary always holy and Mother of God; then, the Holy Spirit is a perfect person; the Trinity forming one God; God glorified with the Father and the Son; and if you renounce the ungodly heresy, then your son will be healed. However, if you persist in this heresy, I myself will pray to the Lord that your son may be taken from life, even before the time fixed for his death has arrived." Emperor Valens, however, remained attached to heresy and said: "I will remain faithful to this belief; but you, who have the power to make my son die or live, make him live and not die." Nerses replied: "I will have mercy on him for fifteen days if you repent; and if you abandon these heresies and these perfidious and impious sects, your son will live." However, the king persisted in his impiety, and fifteen days later the child died, which caused great mourning. Then the emperor brought the holy patriarch before the corpse and said to him: "Resurrect my son, otherwise you will also die." The holy patriarch replied: "I repeat to you, renounce your sect and I, in one day, will resurrect and bring back before you your son."

The emperor did not listen to him and ordered St. Nerses to be tied with iron chains, to be thrown into prison and to be tortured to death there. Then the principals of the city gathered together at the emperor's house and said to him: "We have heard from those who are with him that this man is the kinsman and close friend of their king, and that in their country he is beloved even more than the king. The king [of Armenia] sent him to you for friendship and alliance, and you are destroying him. Then the king of Armenia will wage a terrible war against you." The emperor replied to them: "He is a man equally dangerous to their king and he deserves death. Their king sent him to me to receive death at my hand; he insulted me and killed my son."

St. Nerses stood before the emperor and said: "I die for the name of the Lord, by your hands; but, during this year, you will be struck dead by an invisible sword, and your empire will be given to a man who will carry out the will of my God." The emperor, very irritated, ordered St. Nerses to be exiled to a deserted and distant island, with seventy-two other ecclesiastics, so that they would die there. There was no road by sea which led to this island; there were no roots or water, only sand. The exiles stayed there for about a month and began to suffer from hunger and thirst. Then they rushed to the feet of the man of God, St. Nerses, so that he would provide them with the means of escaping these tortures. St. Nerses began to pray with them. When he had finished his prayer, a wind which rose on the sea, threw on the island an enormous quantity of fish, and also wood and salt. The wood lit itself, without the help of fire. Then St. Nerses began to pray again with everyone; He himself made a hole in the sand, and a spring of fresh water gushed out which lasts to this day. The exiles ate in this way, in the evening of each day. As for St. Nerses, he only ate food every fortnight. They remained on this island for nine months.

Emperor Valens then sent back the princes who accompanied the great Nerses to the king of the Armenians, Arsaces, with titles of honor, money, precious stones and great favors. Having presented themselves before the Emperor Valens, the princes said to him; "We are innocent of the loss of our patriarch, and war may result between us and you." Emperor Valens then wrote to Arsace: "Nerses killed my son, the heir to my empire, and in front of my nobles, he insulted me like a slave; It was because of this that he was exiled, because he deserved to die. Now let not your brotherhood blame me because of him, for if he had acted towards you as he did towards me, you yourself would have taken revenge." He placed all the blame on St. Nerses, wanting by this means to calm King Arsaces.

The princes who had come to the embassy with the great Nerses, took the letter and the large sums of money from Valens, and arrived near Arsaces, in the country of Armenia. When Arsaces learned of the exile of the great Nerses, he became very angry. He ordered Vasag, lord of the Mamigonians, general of the Armenian troops, to form legions, organize an army and march against the country of the Greeks. Vasag the Mamigonian went to the lands of the Greek empire and destroyed from top to bottom a large number of well-defended fortresses in the country; he seized a lot of booty and headed to the shores of the sea, towards the place called Chrysopolis (Khersoubolis). He reduced the city to the last extremity and allowed no one to enter or leave. The Romans did not fight with the Armenians because of the treaty signed between Constantine and the great Tiridates. As for the army which was near Valens, it did not dare to confront the Armenians, because of the power of Vasag. This is why Emperor Valens, finding opposition among the townspeople, withdrew and went to Adrianople (Adrianopolis). Then Patriarch Neetarius, with all the great ones, went to meet Vasag and the Armenian army, and he concluded with them a peace treaty [under which the Armenians agreed] not to devastate the land any further. country and to return peacefully to their homeland. Eight months later, Vasag returned to Arsace with the Armenian army and much loot.

Sometime later, Valens saw in a dream St. Nerses who cut off his head with the sword and said to him: "I am taking your life, because you have darkened many illuminators on earth." The emperor related the dream he had had, and the thing was considered a chimera. The same day, the impious Valens died like a dog, devoured by fire; others say he was killed by an invisible sword. After him, Theodosius, who confessed the Orthodox faith, was placed on the throne. Sailors saw the light of a hearth on the island where St. Nerses was located and Theodosius understood that the great patriarch St. Nerses lived. Immediately he took him home and had the seat of the great Nerses placed above those of all the bishops and even the patriarch, who had gathered on the subject of Macedonius, who rejected the divinity of the Holy Spirit. Emperor Theodosius sent St. Nerses back to the country of Great Armenia, filled with glory and surrounded by great pomp, marks of respect and honor.

IX. At this news, King Arsaces believed that Nerses had risen from the dead, and he went to meet him with his army. His return caused great joy in the country of Armenia. The seat of the holy apostle Thaddeus and the [spiritual] portion of Gregory the Illuminator were renewed. At the time of the great Nerses, all of Armenia resembled a single person of perfect virtue. There were no beggars in his time, because he provided the hospitals with everything the poor needed.

During all the time that St. Nerses had remained away among the Greeks, Arsaces had committed great faults. Having seen an admirable valley, he ordered a city to be built there which he called Arschagavan, and had this edict promulgated in the kingdom: "He who owes something to another, who has kidnapped or the wife of a other, or his servants, his treasures, his horses, his mules, his goods or everything that man covets on earth, if he takes refuge in Arschagavan, he will not be in judgment and no justice will be exercised by royal power." He also had a bridge thrown in a poorly located place, and acted in the same way. The city filled with a considerable number of people, and became a den of criminals, because the bandits, the murderers, the slave thieves, the violators of tombs, in a word all the evildoers, took refuge in this city which provided great income to Arsace.

St. Nerses having learned of the crimes which had been committed in Armenia, entered very irritated to the king and, reprimanding him concerning Arschagavan, he said to him: "Woe to him who builds his residence by injustice, for though there be great and magnificent palaces, yet it will fall into ruin. Now order that this city be demolished, that every inhabitant enter it into his own house; and I will build you other cities with my hands that will produce seven times more money for the royal treasury". The king disdained his advice and took no notice of it. St. Nerses then said to the king: "Since you have not listened to me, God will not listen to you in the day of your distress; since you have no pity on the unfortunate country of Armenia, left without a [spiritual] leader when I went far away to the Greeks, the Lord will not have pity on you in the day of your affliction; since you have denied justice to the sad country of Armenia, royalty will also be taken from the race of Arsaciaes, and you will become the slaves of the satraps of Armenia. You will be mistreated by the very person you mistreated. The Creator will turn his face away from your race, until the arrival of the unclean one from the desert (Antichrist). Your magnificent country will become the prey of foreigners, before your eyes. And you, Arsaces, will be your own executioner in foreign lands, like Saul and Herod, for God has shown me. Since you have committed a new crime, God will send a new punishment to your impure city, and there will not be a stone left there that will not be broken."

St. Nerses also made many other reprimands to the king, and he left him very irritated. The great Nerses went to a solitary place, and there, having begun to pray, God delivered this unjust city to destruction. A pestilential rash formed on men and animals, and they were suddenly struck dead. This evil is called the plague until now. Eighteen thousand houses became deserted. Then, suddenly, a violent earthquake was felt and all the inhabitants were crushed. Nowhere could we see traces of stones or frames [to indicate] that in this place there had existed a city.

After this, St. Nerses left the country of Armenia and went to the city of Edessa (Urrha). When King Arsaces learned of the departure of the saint, he found, among the priests attached to the palace, a man called Schounag. He summoned the bishops of the country so that they ordained him patriarch. The bishops refused, with the exception of the bishop of Kami, Georges; of the bishop of Aghdznik, Dadjad, and the bishop of Antzevatzi, Siméon, who consecrated Schounag as patriarch of Armenia, in place of Nerses. This one did not dare to rebuke the king and consented out of weakness to do all his wishes.

X. Then, the Armenian satraps, the governors of the provinces, the nobles, the heads of families and the people revolted against Arsaces. King Arsace then voluntarily went to find Sapor, king of Persia, accompanied by Vasag the Mamigonian and his three sons, the first of whom was called Manuel and the second Gon. The eldest fled and went to join Nerses in Edessa; his name was Mouschegh the brave. The king of the Persians, Sapor, first received with honor king Arsaces and Vasag the Mamigonian. One day when Arsace was walking in the area to see the horses of King Sapor, a prince (amira), head of the Sapor stables, said to him with a smile: "Rest, king of Armenia, on this pile of grass." Vasag the Mamigonian drew his steel sword and said to him: "This is how you speak to my king!" And, striking him on the shoulder, he split his body in two parts. At this sight, Sapor was astonished and praised Vasag because of his devotion to his master. After that, Sapor, excited by magicians and perfidious men, [to whose speeches] he listened, had Absace chained and taken to Kuzistan (Khoujasdan), to the castle called Anouscli (of Forgetting), where Arsace killed himself with the sword, like Saul and Herod. Thus the word of the man of God, Nerses, was fulfilled for him. Sapor ordered Vasag to be massacred in his prison. As for his sons Manuel, Gon and Hamazasb, he invested them with royal commands at his court.

XI. When the great Nerses learned of the death of Arsaces, he came to find Theodosius, emperor of the Romans, had Bab named king in place of his father Arsaces, and Mouscliegh the brave to replace his father Vasag. Then he took the soldiers of Emperor Theodosius and returned to Armenia. All the Armenians who had dispersed then gathered near the patriarch Nerses, the king and the commander of the army. However, the king of the Persians, Sapor, penetrated into the country of Armenia with his women and with all his forces, and he had pyreas (adrousclian) erected in the churches of the Armenians and Iberians.

Mouscliegh, son of Vasag, general of the Armenians, counted his army and found [that it amounted] to 40,000 [men]. He brought his weapons to Nerses who blessed them; and he prepared to march to meet Sapor. The Armenians no longer had any Roman auxiliaries left. Mouschegli, general of the Armenians, fell upon the army of the Persians, and attacking them with fury, he laid them dead [at his feet]. Sapor took a disguise and fled on a horse. Mouscliegh the Mamigonian took prisoner the great queen Sithilhorag, wife of King Sapor, and his other wives. He also seized a hundred generals, had their skins torn off and filled with grass, and had [these trophies] taken to King Bab. As for King Sapor's wives, he kept them, did not allow anyone to approach them, and sent them back to Sapor. Then, Mouschegh traveled through Armenia and overthrew the Pyreans that were there. By seeing again his women, Sapor was very surprised, and he gave warm thanks to Mouschegh for his generosity. Moushegh's horse was white; Sapor had this painted on a painting and, at rest time, he would get up in front of this image, drink the wine and say: "I drink from the white horse!" Sapor acted in this way because Mouschegh had sent his women back to him, pure of all defilement and without ransom.

When Bab learned that Mouschegh had sent away the wives of the king of the Persians and that he had not brought them to him, he wanted to put him to death; but he did not dare carry out his project, for fear of St. Nerses. After this, the king of the Persians, Sapor, asked for help from the king of the Huns, Urnaïr, and he opened the gates of the Alans. The troops of the Huns, the Massagetes (Mazkliouth), the Akouk, the Lepliin, the Thaumadg, the Koupour, the Djemah, the Koutar, the Ouz, the Djoudj, the Scheghp, the Maghazdj, the Ker, of the Gouan, assembled near him, with other troops belonging to the Pei'se tribes in immense numbers, and to tribes of nomadic Kurdish mountain people. They all arrived together, invaded the plains of Adherbadagan and spread throughout the country of Armenia. The king of the Huns said to the king of the Persians: "I will go against Muschegh with my army, and you, with the troops of the Arik, march against the army of the Greeks." When Manuel the Mamigonièn, brother of Mouschegh the brave, heard these words, he said: "You are going to collect thorns, but it will be wonderful if you manage to collect them." He sent messengers to his brother.

Mouschegh, in order to make him aware of the kings' project. Mouschegh than said: "I trust in the prayers of St. Nerses and their pride will be humbled." The Persian and Roman soldiers were ordered to seize the Romans and take them to their countries to employ them in the palaces and fortresses; but to massacre the Armenian soldiers without pity, in order to exterminate the Armenian race, and so that, he said, they do not constantly keep us in suspense with their attacks.

The love of the Armenians and that of the Gi'ecs meets in the plain of Nebadag with the king of Armenia, Bab; they also bring with them the holy patriarch Nerses. However, Bab did not give Mouschegh the Mamigonian the order to engage in battle, saying: "It is in perspective of this day that Mouschegh delivered Sapor's wife; he must revolt, and he will do our soldiers more harm than the enemies." Mouschegh threw himself at the feet of St. Nerses, and, choosing him as intercessor and mediator, he took his right hand, made solemn oaths, and said: "Never did this idea occur to me the mind, as you believe." St. Nerses said to Bab: "It is I who today make myself the guarantor of his faults." The king, having heard these words, then ordered Mouschegh to engage in combat. St. Nerses watched with them throughout the night and gave communion to those who were worthy [of receiving] the body and blood of the Lord. The brave Mouschegh brought his war armor and his weapons to St. Nerses, so that he would give them to him himself. All the Armenian and Greek generals also present their weapons to St. Nerses so that he may bless them with the sign of the cross he blesses their weapons by signing them with the sign of the cross. Mouschegh took the scarf of St. Nerses, tied it to the end of his spear and marched into battle. Then St. Nerses reached the summit of Mount Nebad, stretched out his pure hands towards heaven, and, still holding them elevated, he prayed to God.

General Mouschegh preceded the Greek army with the Armenian army and arrived before it in front of the enemy troops; and, like the fire which violently devours the reeds, he separated the army of the Persians from that of the Huns. When Bab saw the banner of Mouschegh disappear, he said to St. Nerses: "Woe! it was you who was the cause of the massacre of the Armenian army by the ferocious Moushegh!" St. Nerses replied to the king: "Do not think that, O king! of the faithful and loyal race of the Mamigonians; on the contrary you will appreciate its value today." Bab replied to St. Nerses: "Pray to God without ceasing, O holy patriarch! implore him out loud." The latter, raising his hands, recited this prayer with great sighs:

"Lord, Almighty God, hear my prayer that your name may be glorified; for, although impiety reigns in the country of Armenia, you nevertheless have the power to punish faults on all occasions; but in this day turn not your face from us, and spare your people whom you have redeemed with your divine blood."

However [Nerses] addressed these prayers to God, invoking the help of a merciful God. The armies, having attacked each other from both sides, struck each other fiercely, like the hammers of blacksmiths and the shrill blows of woodcutters. When this great melee was even more complete, the Armenian army routed the troops of the Alans, Persians, Uz and Massagetae. But when St. Nerses lowered his hands, the fugitives stopped and again offered resistance to the Armenians, and when the saint stretched out his hands, the troop of infidels dispersed before the Armenian army. After that, the Armenian soldiers pursued the fugitives and massacred almost all the infidels.

The king of the Persians, Sapor, dismounting, changed his clothes and escaped death by hiding in a cave. The general of the Armenians, Mouschegh, lord of the Mamigonians, having reached Ournaïr, king of the Huns, struck him on the head with the shaft of his spear and said to him: "Behold, I am the rival you were looking for, but congratulate you to be king, because I do not give death to crowned heads. I am Mouschegh the Mamigonian whom you were looking for in single combat." Having spoken in this way, he let him continue on his way and did not take him near Bab, so that the latter would not kill him. After this terrible and murderous combat in which they had won the victory, the Armenian and Greek armies joined King Bab and the patriarch Nerses with immense booty and great testimonies of joy.

In this battle, no soldier of the Armenian army died. Mouschegh the Mamigonian recounted a marvelous fact; it is that, during the heat of the combat, there was, [he said], between the enemies and us such dust and such shadow caused by the arrows which rose above us in the air, such lowings of elephants and such a sound of spears in the darkness, that no one knew how to distinguish their own from the enemies. Then the holy patriarch walked before us and showed us with his hand our enemies, on whom we fell, making them bite the dust. The whole army related this vision in the same way, and all, prostrating themselves at the feet of St. Nerses, said to him: "Victory is yours!" They then came down from the mountain and celebrated a great festival the same day.

At the same time, some denouncers appeared before King Bab and told him: "General Mouschegh has seized the king of the Alans, Ournaïr, has taken him prisoner and has not brought him to you. Nor did he take his life, but let him go safely, as [he did] with the wives of King Sapor." Hearing these words, King Bab turned his face away from Mouschegh, looked at him with an evil eye and sought the opportunity to put him to death. When Moushegh appeared before King Bab, he said to him: "Why do you turn your face away from me? Have I committed an act of cowardice? I have killed a number of my equals that I do not know; but he was a king, and, although he is unfaithful, it is up to you to kill him, because he is your equal. As for me, I will never lay a hand on him, and it will never happen to me to strike a man who has been anointed, as long as I live. Here I am now in your presence; kill me, if you want, for I am ready to receive death at your hands." King Bab embraced Mouschegh tightly and said to him: "Those who slandered Mouschegh deserve death." The king gave him many presents, and Mouschegh said to the king: "From now on I will shed my blood for Armenia; but you, O king! see with your eyes and hear with your ears, and do not rely on the testimony of others. Distinguish the good from the bad, the worthy man from the worthless, and the country of Armenia will be on the right track." The king listened to these words and they pleased him.

The Armenian general, Mouschegh, left this place and, with the help of the Armenian army, put up strong resistance to all attacks. For his part, the great Nerses visited the entire country of Armenia and gathered everywhere the fruits of his preaching. His disciple Mesrob, who was called Maschtotz, accompanied him: he had given himself over to all the practices of spiritual things, devoted himself to mortification, taking no rest during the night, and employing the time spent sleeping to waking up. He led this existence for a long time.

XII. However, King Bab indulged in debauchery; St. Nerses reprimanded him, but he did not listen. St. Nerses then turned his face away from him and cursed him as he had cursed his father Arsaces. Immediately the devs began to torment the king, and they appeared to him in the form of snakes. Bab then came and threw himself at the feet of St. Nerses and requested his forgiveness so that he would come to his home. When the great Nerses entered his home, the king was relieved and found rest; the devs no longer showed themselves to him and fled from him; but when Nerses left, King Bab was again tormented by the fire of his passions. St. Nerses prayed and the devs fled; but when the saint left, the king fell back into the same tortures. Then St. Nerses forbids him from entering the Church; but the king sought a favorable opportunity to kill Nerses, without daring to accomplish his project for fear of the satraps and the people who came to the patriarch. Indeed, the sick found healing and became the disciples of Nerses, and a large number of people did not leave him. St. Nerses also healed, by making with his hand the sign of the cross, the new scourge with which God struck the guilty city of Arschagavan and which is called plague until today.

After that, King Bab treacherously invited the great Nerses to a feast, at the village of Ivhakh, in the canton of Egeghiatz, in order to put him to death by poison. The king said treacherously to him: "If you eat with me, I will behave from now on forever according to your will, and I will do what you command me. I will do penance with hair shirt and ashes according to your desire." St. Nerses, unaware that he was plotting his downfall, went with him to the feast. When they entered the room, the king forced him to sit on the royal throne, but Nerses did not consent, and it was only after strong insistence that he sat on the king's seat. King Bab stood up, stripped himself of his clothes, came down from his seat, poured him a drink, and, throwing poison into the cup, he presented it to the saint. When Nerses had drunk, he thanked [God] saying: "Blessed be you, O God, that you have judged me worthy to drink the cup of martyrdom, and to suffer for you this death which I have desired since my childhood. However, I did not seek death of my own free will; because if we throw ourselves into it without necessity, it is pride, and He who rewards does not accuse the presumptuous, because he is condemned to give in like Peter. As for you, unjust king! We only use poison and trickery against those we cannot seize, while I was constantly with you. Who then held back your hand to kill me openly? Lord! forgive them for what they have done to me without cause, and receive the soul of your servant, you who give peace to all your servants." He got up and returned to his monastery.

All the princes and all the Armenian generals, Muschegh, the Martbed who is called father of the king (thakavorhaïr), the nobles, the provincial governors, followed him in mourning and were overwhelmed with sadness. The saint, having entered his monastery and having taken up his cloak, [it was noticed] that he had bluish spots the size of a cake at the place of his heart. The satraps presented him with antidotes and counter-poison to combat the effect of the venom and save him; but Nerses refused, so as not to make himself unworthy of the divine mystery and the salutary body of the Lord, and he said: "Let me promptly abandon this unjust world and these ungrateful men. The separation of soul and body is terrible, and it will be even more frightening when, after the resurrection, we are given over to torments; because the first disunites the bonds of the soul and the body, while the second openly proclaims sins. Indeed, it is not possible for the one who has committed injustice to hide, and his sins will be held against him before the impartial tribunal. But you, O righteous God, show me your mercy and have mercy on me!

"When the trumpet sounds and the heavenly armies raise their voices, then the unfortunate are lost in their anxiety and they are claimed by hell, while the cohorts of the righteous sing in chorus with the seraphim. Lord, please have mercy on me and have mercy on me!"

"When I hear the terrible sound of the trumpet in the last day, I will sit with you in the judgment seat, and all, Lord, will gather before you for the terrible judgment; then my bones crack, my mind can no longer think, I condemn myself in my mind and say to myself: "How will I be saved?" But, O God, because of my repentance and my penance, have pity on me and show me mercy!"

When the people heard these words, they began to shed bitter tears. Mouschegh the Mamigonian, Haïr le martbed, Pagour, prince of the Iberians, the prince of the Pakradouni, Haïg of the race of Haïg, Méroujan, prince of the Ardzrouni, Hamam, prince of Melitene, and the other great princes and satraps, the chiefs of race and the governors of the provinces of the country of Armenia, as well as the bishops, implored him to take the antidote. But the holy patriarch refused, saying: "I can, of my own accord with the help of my God, drive out suffering from my body, but I prefer to endure them so as not to stop in the path that God traced me; for the chief of the martyrs calls me to receive the reward for my labors. But, since the race of the Arsacids was exterminated in the country of Armenia many illuminators of my race extinguished the divine light which was in it. The Lord will destroy them as he did Israel. As for what they did to me, may it be forgiven for them; for my wish has been fulfilled. When fifty years have passed, the priesthood will be taken from our family which is that of my ancestor St. Gregory, and the royalty will also be torn from the race of the Arsacids, when the impious one of the desert will have approached. Then, when a hundred and fifty years have passed, the Persians will take possession of the holy city of Jerusalem, of the Cross, and they will lead it into captivity, and when it leaves the Persians, it will no longer return to Jerusalem. The holy city will no longer remain in the power of the Greeks; the Ismailites will seize it, impose tribute on the Greeks until the time when the nation of the brave approaches. Then Jerusalem will be taken by the nation of the Romans, who are called the Franks, and they will deliver the Greeks from their tribute.

XIII. "Now, the ruin of the provinces of Armenia will be brought about by the cunning and disobedience of some towards others: the princes will not obey the sovereign and will each retire to their province; they will not help each other and will instead side with the enemies. Then everyone will abandon their inheritance, and all will fall under the yoke of the Greeks, in their slavery and servitude; they will relax in their faith, and their power will be weakened accordingly. The Greek monarchs lived a short time; they will not concern themselves with war, but with taxes, with the change of [religious] institutions, with the examination of the faith that the three apostolic councils have established; they will shake the Christian belief of a crowd of people, and that will be the focus of their efforts and concerns. The Greek warriors will lose their energy; their country will be oppressed by the nation of archers (Turks); they will fall under their yoke, and many provinces will become deserted. The world will be in anxiety; there will be fires, floods and earthquakes. Many cities will collapse, and wonders and phenomena will appear in all countries.

"The priesthood will be interrupted for several years in Armenia; and the country will be shaken from top to bottom; inaccessible fortresses will be stormed by the nation of archers. The men of this nation will devour the flesh of their arms, that is to say of their fellow citizens, according to the prophecy of Isaiah and the words of John who says: "There are many antichrists in the world." The holy places of the seats of the patriarchy will become the residences and habitations of the pagan nations; the busy roads will become deserted by the lack of men; help will no longer come from any side. Then they will say to the mountains: "Fall on us, and to the hills. Cover us," according to Jeremiah's prophecy. Charity will dry up among many people and, on the contrary, harshness will take root among them; men will be in anxiety, and the whole earth will become anxious and agitated; educated people will take refuge in the regions of the East.

"Then, all Christian countries will be saved by the brave Roman armies. The world will live in peace and be on the right path for a long time; it will become like a garden producing all things abundantly. The infidels will be pushed back and will fall under the yoke of Roman servitude. Men will pity those who preceded them in life and those who did not benefit from all these felicities. Finally, the son of perdition, the Antichrist, will appear."

"However, while I still live, I make known to you, the coming [of the Antichrist] will be brought about by the power of Satan. It will not be over the Arabs (Dadjik), nor over the Persians, nor even over the pagans that he will reign, but over the servants of the triumphant cross; for he also, the son of perdition, will be lost through the glory [of the cross]. This impure being will be a reproach for the Jews who await this corrupter. But as for you, command your sons, and let your sons command their sons, to write [all this], to preserve it until the coming of the unclean, that they may be prepared against their pitfalls and that they do not allow themselves to be surprised.

"I have given you [spiritual life] through the pool of light (baptism), and, until my last breath, I am full of tenderness for you; However, I fear that some vice will take root in your children after I leave this world. May God, Word of the Father, lead in my place his people whom he has redeemed with his blood! The sign of the coming of the Antichrist will be this: when after happy times the world is given over to discord, the kingdom of the Greeks will be destroyed, just as it was revealed to Daniel, in the form of four beasts fierce, namely the lioness, which is the kingdom of the Medes, the bear, that of the Babylonians, the leopard, that of the Persians, and the fourth, which was terrible and frightening to see, the one who devoured and devastated the earth, the kingdom of the Greeks. Likewise, by the coming of Christ, the kingship of Israel was destroyed, and thus, at the coming of the unclean one, the power of the Greeks will be destroyed. The three kingdoms were annihilated, and the fourth, which held strong, and which is the Greek power, will be destroyed by the Antichrist."

"Before that, harshness will dominate, and charity will dry up; there will be famines, earthquakes and great mortality. The brother will deliver his brother to death and the father his son, as the Lord said, as you know, and the earth will grow cold. What you sow will not be reaped, and what you plant will not be eaten, and there will be many wonders when the Antichrist comes. Do not believe that it is Satan or a demon of his legions; he is a man of perverse spirit from the tribe of Dan; he will be born in the village of Khorazin, of the race of Israel; the name of his father is Hrovméla and that of his mother Nerghiminè, and he will be called Hi'asim. Ilseranouri'i by virgins and will go to Byzantium where he will grow in reputation among the dignities in Greece. Then the kingdom of the Greeks will be divided into ten parts. He will become one of the kings, put to death three of the sovereigns, seize the persons of the others and establish his domination over everyone. His reign will be three and a half years. He will ravage the earth in anger; he will have in his wake all the satellites of Satan, because his coming comes from the very power of Satan. He will perform miracles for one thousand two hundred and sixty days. But hey to them who will have shown patience and will reach the Days of Our Lord and Savior Jesus Christ! At that time, if two people grind in the same mill, one will be left, the other will be left; the leaves of the fig tree beginning to grow signify the Antichrist; the growth of the branches means the satellites; the mill is life, and whoever is caught is the choice of the good among the bad.

"Then the son of perdition will sit in the Church of God; he will begin to blaspheme God and he will demand that we pay homage to him as to God. He will pretend to be God and he will be proud before all those who bear the name of God. Alone, he pretends to be worshiped in place of God and he will fill the world with evil and filth. God will then send his two prophets, Enoch and Elijah, to deliver men. They will protect the faithful and will turn the hearts of the fathers to their sons, as the Lord has said with his mouth: "Elijah will come and make straight the ways before me." Now, as John was the precursor of Christ during his first appearance, so it is reserved for Elijah and Enoch to be his precursors at his second appearance. They will all come and will say: "Do not believe in the unclean one who dwells in the holy place, for he is the great dragon and the crooked serpent; he seduces you with deception and false miracles; do not approach him but flee to the mountains. Be patient for a while; it is the false Christ, and, through false prophets, he wants to deceive the servants of the cross, and he is the inspiration of several errors. Pray day and night, for prayer is little and the reward will be eternal."

"As for Christ, he will not come from earth, but from heaven, surrounded by unspeakable glory, and he will plunge [the Antichrist] into deep darkness and cruel toils. Christ will not come before Pilate to be judged, but on the contrary, it will be he who will judge the world. Enoch and Elijah will prophesy these and similar things to men. Then the earth will become corrupted and impure by the odor of dead bodies, and it will be corrupted on every side. The faces of humans will decay from the tortures of famine and thirst for water. Gold, precious stones, coats of various colors will be scattered on the ground, and no one will want to possess them for fear of the dangers with which we are threatened in these times of calamity. It is then those men, the corrupt people, will remember their guilty actions, those who had themselves marked on their foreheads with the seal of impiety, and they will say to the Antichrist: "Help us in our torments, because we will all die." But he will not come to their aid; and he will deceive them with false promises. He will then seize Enoch and Elijah, and this impure being will make them endure terrible torments and will continue to blaspheme God many times. When the holy prophets have despised his deceptions and false signs, he will put Enoch and Elijah to death in the presence of a great multitude of people, and the false prophets will rejoice when they see the death of the true prophets. It is then that the great dragon, the father of perdition himself, will make it loud in the ears of all: "Behold my power! These (Enoch and Elijah) were immortal for a long series of years, they could not escape from my hands, and no one could overcome my power." He will further multiply crime on the earth, and the Lord Jesus will destroy it with the breath of his mouth. He will blaspheme the Most High in the presence of many people. But when he speaks like this, suddenly, in the blink of an eye, we will hear a great rolling of

thunder, and at the same time the satellites of the impure Antichrist will disappear and perish. Then the Lord will shine the royal and luminous sign, to encourage those who have had recourse to him, to the glory of the righteous, because they have attached themselves to the cross with sincere love. The parts of this almighty sign and the forces of the Holy Church will be reflected and take on the dimension of the cross of the Lord, and the stars will be darkened by its light. The nations will lament, for the Lord will come to judge those who have not been confirmed by [the sign of the cross] and who have not recognized it.

"Then the resplendent King will descend from heaven in his unspeakable glory; the earth will tremble and melt like wax before the fire. Dark rivers, rolling flames, will fall from heights and purify the earth of impieties and impurities. The celestial legions will make their voices heard, the heavens will shake, and the trumpet will sound loudly in the tombs: "Arise, dead, and run to meet the bridegroom, for he has come with glory from his father; arise, ye righteous and sinners, and come and receive your reward." Then the creatures who had not prepared themselves will lament in despair and hastily put on their bodily covering. The bodies of sinners will appear dark, for they will be tarnished by their evil deeds; the elect will go before them and their bodies will become luminous; they will rise from the earth in a resplendent cloud before Christ, and the heavenly inhabitants will look upon them and say: "What have they done on earth to come thus in joyful groups to meet the Lord?" The Lord will answer them: "These are my faithful champions who have renounced themselves, distanced themselves from the world, and crucified their bodies through deprivation and pain. Because of their love for me, I will now give them everlasting joy." When the angels hear these words, they will say: "You are blessed by the Lord, rejoice." Then the King of glory will sit on his throne, and the angels will serve him with fear. Satan will be the first to be chained without judgment and he will be thrown into the abyss of Tartarus. His satellites of the left, who have taught men evil deeds, will be tied with terrible bonds and will not be judged worthy to appear before the tribunal [of the Lord], because they will not be able to justify themselves, and immediately they will move away from him. The righteous, full of hope of reward, will stand at his right hand and the sinners will also line up there, covered with shame, to answer for their actions. A tribunal will be formed, the books will be opened, the condemned men will be gathered together as if in bundles, and they will be thrown into the inextinguishable fire. As for the others, the doors [of the house] of joyful weddings will be closed to them, so that they cannot see the celestial bridegroom; for the lamps of mercy will not be lit for them and they will be told: "I do not know you, depart from me." But, before all this, the king will give the celestial crown to those who have deserved it, saying to them: "Come, my Father's elect, take your place in paradise, which has been prepared for you from the beginning of the world."

"Then the heavens will be renewed, the earth will also be renewed and will be covered with pleasant greenery. Paradise will produce thirty to one, as the earthly paradise will produce sixty to one and the heavens will produce a hundred to one. There will be no more labor or fatigue on earth, no deceitful serpent, no seductive woman; but on the contrary there will be trees with inexhaustible fruit. There will be no more sorrow or sadness, but only joy and gladness. To some, the Lord will give paradise on earth. The martyrs will wear crowns that will shine in the color of purple, like their cloaks and their glory. It will be the same for virgins who have not been defiled by contact with the world; They will receive with the Virgin Mary the splendor of the crown of glory and will be like the sun in the middle of the stars. Thus the glory of virgins will be greater than that of married couples."

"You, my sons, understand all these things that you may avoid the snares of the hunter, and escape the snares like the deer, and you will be my glory in the day of the Lord [by placing yourselves] in his right hand, as the Lord made me see it."

XIV. St. Nerses, after having predicted all these things with a prophetic eye, and after the people and the great satraps of Armenia had listened to him, experienced terrible pains. Mouschegh the Mamigonian and the other princes threw themselves at the feet of the saint and asked him for forgiveness [of their sins] and his blessing. He freed them [from their sins] and entrusted them to God and to the Word of his grace. Then he called near him General Mouschegh and the other princes of the Mamigonian family who were present, and laying his hands on them, he blessed them thus:

"May the Lord God," he said, "be the guide of the Mamigonians, as he was of king David and of general Joshua. May He establish your feet unshakably and strengthen your hands against your enemies. The first blessings which were said: "One person will hunt a thousand, and two will hunt ten thousand, and will be given to the family of the Mamigonians. You will be blessed among all the families of the earth. You will stand firm in the orthodox faith; you will be renowned, and you will triumph with the Christian faith. You will not fall under the yoke of the pagans, and the salvation of the nations will be effected by you. Precious pearls will be chosen from among the members of the Mamigonian family and will be placed on the crown of Christ, because of their martyrdom." He blessed them by speaking other words.

After this, the saint raised his hands which had always been extended for a whole hour, in favor of the country of Armenia; he implored God and said: "Lord God, most compassionate and most merciful, preserve without stain the faith of the country of Armenia through the intercession of the holy apostle Thaddeus to whom this country fell in share, and of my ancestor Gregory, his imitator; for, although there is impiety among the Armenian people who follow the example of their ancestors, strike them with your mercy, and ensure that no heresy contrary to the holy faith enters into the country of Armenia, may no raging torrent defile the incorruptible chalice of your altar and the sacred bread of your salutary mystery. I pray to you, Lord, to preserve the Armenians in the purity of the true faith and to prevent hungry wolves from approaching the entrance to your holy flock. Keep your share in the apostolic faith, so that the disciples of error, the troops of heretics, convert the superb minds of their disciples, whose pride the light of your Gospel has not been able to lower. But if, by surprise and by the force of the devil, heretics introduce themselves into this division, I pray to you, Lord, to uproot them entirely from this country. May no trouble come to disturb the source of pure water which springs from the current of your divinity in the land of Armenia and preserve this sharing in all its purity until your second coming."

After having said this prayer, the holy patriarch entered the church, bade farewell to the holy altar and to all the brothers who were present and spoke thus: "Farewell, holy church, farewell, holy altar; farewell, ecclesiastical orders, my brothers, believing in the Lord; farewell war cohorts, warriors, farewell, ministers and readers of the holy Church; goodbye everyone! I moved towards my Creator; I have abandoned my entire existence, my entire heritage, and, according to your orders, I am ready to return to the earth with which I was created. Behold, I separate myself from you, holy Church, behold, I separate myself from you, my beloved brothers, at the call of Christ, my God, who has made all things new. Pray for me, my fathers, my brothers and my sons, and Christ our Savior will bless you; he will keep you faithful in the faith until the appointed time; May the peace of the Lord be with you forever. Amen!"

Then he sat down on his patriarchal seat and said: "You have anointed my forehead with oil, your drink has intoxicated me like pure wine."

"When the body departs from life, after death all thoughts are annihilated; even at that moment all bodily combat also ceases, because we have arrived at the knowledge of the things which are going to be accomplished. Then we are frightened, and we tremble in front of the court; the acts of each person are listed, for each man is judged worthy of reward according to his actions. You (who are still powerful and who has the power [to judge] after death, have pity on me, during the terrible judgment, and have mercy on me! When [I reflect] that the human race will gather before you, my my bones tremble, and your threats cause me terrible terror, O heavenly King! for I have accumulated many impieties and sins, and yet I call on you to my help; you who can do everything, and who are the physician of souls, O Lord, have mercy on me!"

Sweat drenched his body, the illness caused him horrible suffering, and he strode towards rest. Rising from his seat, he walked towards the entrance of the church, raised his hands, looked at the sky with a joyful heart and recalled in his prayers all the distant or neighboring countries. His disciple Mesrob, who was later called Maschotz, listened to his words. He prayed again and said: "My person has come near to the earth from which I was created. Since I sinned and committed offenses against the commandments, I experienced a cruel death; Lord, my hope, help me! We ask you for mercy, King of kings, Lord of Lords, when the angelic cohorts and powers come to meet you and you appear in great glory and with the sound of the trumpet to awaken those who sleep and heal those who are injured. Then you will come with lightning, you will judge by unquenchable fire, you will appear in the heavens, towards the east, and the holy cross will appear radiant before you. You will make yourself visible to the world and you will judge everyone according to their actions. The books will be opened, the seats will be placed, and an impartial judgment will be rendered. Scales will be ready for the righteous and for sinners. The great sound of trumpets will be heard, the powers will run and the angels will be filled with fear. The fire will shine, the sun and the moon will be darkened, the stars will fall, the clouds will merge, the sea will dry up and all creatures will be plunged into amazement. The good will rejoice, the wicked will lament, the martyrs will be crowned according to their merits, and the executioners will be punished for their cruelties. The renegades will be devoured by thirst; those who are crucified will be condemned, and those who worship the cross will rejoice. The renegades will lament; those who deserve crowns will shine, and the virgins will rejoice. The nuptial chamber will be decorated, and the wise virgins, who have prepared themselves, will enter with lit lamps, while the foolish virgins, who remain outside with extinguished lamps, their heads bowed, their hearts saddened, will be driven out by the voice of the king who will say: "I do not know you." Those on the right will rejoice and those on the left will weep. The lambs will leap, and the goats will be rejected from the face of the Lord. The light will shine in all its splendor, the darkness will diminish, hell will cry out and Satan will be covered in confusion; our ambition will pass and the worm will not die.

"Now when all this is accomplished by your power, then place and exalt the soul of your servant in the shining mansions, with the martyrs, with those who have fulfilled your commandments and who have believed in you through your word. I, humble as I am and who occupied the seat of the apostle Thaddeus and my [ancestor] St. Gregory, who spent my days with joy, without passion, according to your wishes, in the way he told you pleased, Lord Jesus Christ, now receive my soul in peace!"

Having pronounced these words, he ordered the people to depart from him, and, while praying, the holy patriarch Nerses gave up the ghost, confessing the Father, the Son and the Holy Spirit, in the month of Hroditz, the day of Thursday. The people did not notice the death of the man of God, because his hands were extended towards the sky and his neck was straight. Then they approached him to make him sit down because he was tired, and his person was languid from the pain of the poison. But when they saw that he was dead, everyone was amazed; They threw themselves on his neck and began to shout loudly. The land of Armenia resounded with cries and groans because the blood of the righteous had been shed in vain. The saint was placed, with great lamentations, on his patriarchal seat, and he seemed to those who looked at him as a living person.

Two solitaires, one called Epiphanes, the other Scliaghida, who had retired, the first to the mountain of Arioudz (Lion), and the second to Nébadag, and other fathers who lived in caves and in caverns, at the moment when St. Nerses left life, everyone saw, in their solitude, during the day, the great Nerses, as if transported with his body into the heavens in the middle of the clouds. The angels supported him, presented themselves before him in hurried groups, offering him crowns of light brighter than the sun. At this sight, the holy fathers, at the height of astonishment and stupor, came to the canton of Egeghiatz, in the village of Khakh, and learned of the death of the holy man of God, the great Nerses; they shed abundant tears and said: "O illuminator of the world! who has not sinned and who, through your innocence and your fervent prayers, has thawed the ice of the sins of the guilty, remember us before God!" The holy anchorites related their vision to the people, which caused great astonishment. After this, the king and the other great princes arranged a coffin, and, having placed the saint in it, they buried him in the village called Thil. For forty days, a column of light was seen on his tomb; many healings were carried out at his tomb and even until today; because, by taking earth from his tomb, one was cured of the disease called the plague, a new and terrible disease which he himself asked of God to punish Arsehagavan, a guilty city and home of iniquity.

This was how the great Nerses lived during his life, and this is how he died, after leading, with the Orthodox faith, the Patriarchate of Great Armenia for thirty-four years.

XV. Then the satraps, the princes, the nobles and the sabrag of the country of Armenia, gathered in one place and they mutually consoled each other for the death of the saint. They believed in an elder and entrusted her to Mouschegh the Mamigonian, to prepare for the battles. Mouschegh told them: "I cannot [accept], because we will no longer have victory. Our triumph came through the prayers of the saint, and it seems to my mind that Armenia has been abandoned by God, for the righteous are no more, and who now will pray for us?" Everyone agreed with his opinion.

Although Bab had killed Nerses, he could not be satisfied with these crimes. He ordered the destruction of the monasteries, hospitals and all buildings built by Blessed Nerses. When the satraps saw this behavior, they resolved to kill Bab and to elevate the brave Mouscbegli to royal dignity. But he distracted them from this thought and said to them: "Have you not heard St. Nerses ordering us and telling us not to avenge his death, because it is up to the Lord to do so? punish her?"

However, when Emperor Theodosius heard that the Armenian king Bab had put St. Nerses to death, he secretly sent a letter to the Greek general who had come to the aid of the Armenians, to find a way to kill Bab. The general invited the king of Armenia Bab to a feast, and he hid in the house legionaries carrying naked swords in their hands. When the guests were under the influence of the vapors of the wine, the soldiers surrounded Bab and killed him on the table. This prince had reigned over Great Armenia for seven years. This vengeance was exercised by the Lord, because of the man of God, the great Nerses.

From the moment of the death of St. Nerses, war and internal divisions did not cease in the country of Armenia. After the death of King Bab, General Mouschegh united the Armenian army and made frequent incursions into the country of the Persians. The prisoners he took had their skin torn off, and they filled it with grass, saying: "Be immolated to [the memory] of Arsace and my father Vasag. "He traveled the country, destroyed the pyreas which were in the country of Armenia and in Iberia and he restored the churches."

After these events, Theodosius the Great ascended the throne of Armenia, in place of his cousin (son of his father's brother) Bab, Varaztad. Moushegh was slandered before the king, saying that it was he who had been the cause of Bab's death. King Varaztad wanted to put Mouschegh to death, but he could not succeed, because of the power of Mouschegh and for fear of the princes of Armenia. However, he invited Mouschegh to a feast, and when he sat down and the guests were intoxicated by the fumes of the wine, twenty men whom he had hidden suddenly entered and grabbed Mouschegh by both hands. , while King Varaztad hastily pierced his heart with his spear. Moushegh said: "For what purpose are you doing this?" Varaztad replied: "Go and ask Bab why you delivered him into the hands of his murderers." Moushegh continued: "Here then is the reward for my services, for my fatigue, demon blood, for my sweat which I wiped with my spear instead of using a cloth. Bless God! but why did I not die on horseback in the battles I fought for the Christians?" Sempad, prince of the Sahrouni, drawing his sword, thrust it into the throat of Mouschegh. His body was taken and taken to the canton of Daron, and buried in the convent of Glag. King Varaztad appointed Sempad Sahrouni general in place of Mouschegh.

By an effect of divine providence, the king of Persia sent back to their homeland Manuel and Gon, sons of Vasag the Mamigonian and brothers of general Mouschegh, who had been assassinated. They had been taken captive by the Arsaces and with their father Vasag the Mamigonian. Manuel, who was of high stature, and his brother Gon, son of Vasag, came to their canton of Daron and settled there. The blessing of St. Nerses was accomplished in favor of the family of the Mamigonians; Manuel and Gon extended their domination over several cantons; Manuel seized command of the army from Sempad Sahrouni and took the place of his brother Mouschegh and his father Vasag.

Manuel sent the following message to Varaztad: "My race shed its blood for the royalty of the Arsacids, for the holy churches and the orthodox faith; thus, my grandfather Vatché for Chosroès, my father Vasag for Arsace, and my brother Mouschegh for Bab. But you, instead of doing good to the faithful family of the Mamigonians, you caused them a lot of harm: my brother Mouschegh, a strong and brave man in God, whom the enemies could not defeat, you took and cruelly massacred him. ¬ lies, without any reason, like a worthless man. You certainly know that the Mamigonian race was never under your control, but that [its members were] your companions. Our ancestors, the kings of the Djen, who are our ancestors, that is to say grandparents, were both sons of the king of the Djen. They fled, came to settle in the country of Armenia, and they were honored by the king as companions. The name of the eldest was Mam, and that of the second Gon, and of these two [names, their descendants] were called Mamigon. But you, Varaztad, are not an Arsacid, but a bastard. Leave the country of Armenia if you do not want to perish by my hand to wash away the blood of my brother Moushegh." Varaztad sent to Manuel, general of Armenia and prince of the Mamigonians, an insolent response, in these terms: "What you say, that you are the grandson [of the king] of the Djen, is true. Well, return to your country of Djen, otherwise you will also die by my hand like the perfidious Mouschegh your brother." When Manuel, general of Armenia, read the king's letter, he united the army of Great Armenia. King Varaztad organized his troops and called on the Greek army for help. When the messages ceased from both sides, the two armies came to camp on the plain of Garin. After the two troops came to blows, the king's army and that of the Greeks were defeated. The Annenie general Manuel and his son Hemaïag reached King Varazfad; Hemaïag, son of Manuel the Mamigonian, threw the king off his mount and wanted to kill him; but Manuel prevented him, and, after striking the king on the head, they returned full of joy to their camp. King Varaztad fled to the country of the Greeks and died there soon after.

Manuel governed the country of Armenia with his three sons for several years. The names of his sons were: the eldest Hemaïag, the second Ardavazt, and the third Hamazasb.

Then, General Manuel took the wife of the king of Armenia Bab, who was called Zarmantoukhd, with the two sons she had from King Bab; he kept them holy according to the Christian religion, and he raised them as [befits] the sons of a king. They then ascended the royal throne of their fathers, the Arsacids.

Finally, Manuel left the world by his death; he was taken away and buried in the canton of Daron of Great Armenia, at the monastery of Glag.

St. Sahag the Parthian had no son, but a daughter called Saliaganousch, who was given in marriage to Hamazasb, prince of the Mamigonians, son of Manuel. From Hamazasb, were born St. Vartan and the glorious Hemaïag who were illustrious in Christ our Lord, to whom belong the glory, the power and the triumph, now, always and eternally. Amen!

The Scriptorium Project is the work of a small group of lay people of various apostolic churches who are interested in the preservation, transmission, and translation of the works of the early and medieval church. Our efforts are to make the works of the church fathers accessible to anyone who might have an interest in Christian antiquities and the theological, philosophical, and moral writings that have become the bedrock of Western Civilization.

To-date, our releases have pulled from the Greek, Syriac, Georgian, Latin, Celtic, Ethiopian, and Coptic traditions of Christianity, and have been pulled from sundry local traditions and languages.

Other Selections from the Armenian Church Series:

Refutations by Eznik of Kolb (Dec. 2007)

Explanation of the Faith of the Armenian Church by Nerses IV the Gracious, Catholicos of Armenia (July 2009)

The Life of Mashtots by Koriun the Iberian (Nov. 2012)

Letter to Kiwron, Catholicos of Iberia by Movses II, Catholic of Armenia (Nov. 2013)

Canons of the Synod of Partav by Sion I, Catholicos of Armenia (Dec. 2013)

The History of the Holy Cross of Aparank by St. Gregory of Narek (Feb. 2014)

Armenian Synaxarium: Volume I- Month of Navasard (Oct. 2018)

The Geography by Ananias of Shirak (Dec. 2020)

Genealogy of the Family of St. Gregory by St. Mesrop Mashtots (Nov. 2023)

www.ingramcontent.com/pod-product-compliance
Lightning Source LLC
LaVergne TN
LVHW061042070526
838201LV00073B/5148